All the Way to God

by Katie and Michael Giuliano

illustrated by

The Giuliano Children

A Golden Book • New York
Golden Books Publishing Company, Inc.
New York, New York 10106

I'll never forget the night
I told my daddy how much
I REALLY loved him.
All my brothers were running around,
getting ready for bed.
I finished first and got under the covers.

I waited for my daddy to tuck me in, always with a kiss and a question. "Goodnight, Katie. How much does Daddy love you?" he asked.

"You love me this much, Daddy!"
I stretched my arms
as far as I could.
"But, Daddy, I love you even more.
I love you all the way to the ceiling."

Daddy looked a little surprised.
I'd never tried to top his love before.
"Well, Katie, if you love me
all the way to the ceiling,
then I love you
all the way to the roof."

"Daddy, if you love me
all the way to the roof,

then I love you all the way
to the top of the trees!"

Daddy didn't even blink
when he said, "If you love me
all the way to the top of the trees,
then I love you
all the way up to the clouds."

This game was getting to be fun!

"Daddy, if you love me
all the way up to the clouds,
then I love you all the way to the sky."

"Katie, if you love me
all the way to the sky,
then I love you all the way
to the satellites in space."
I wasn't too sure how far that was,
but I could go even further.

"Daddy, if you love me
all the way to the satellites in space,
then I love you
all the way to the moon."

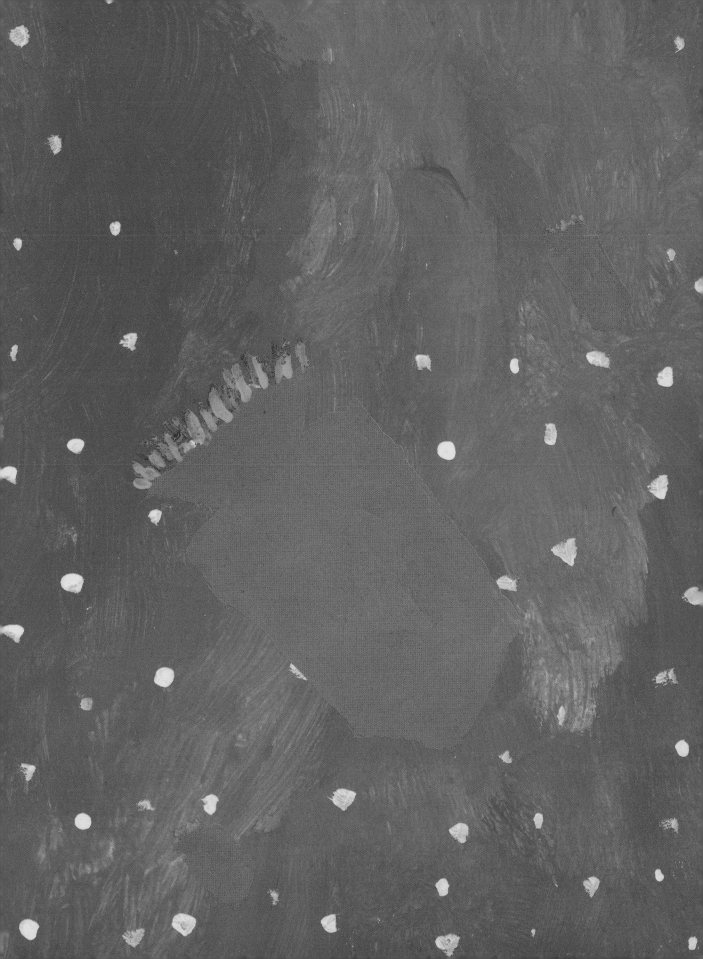

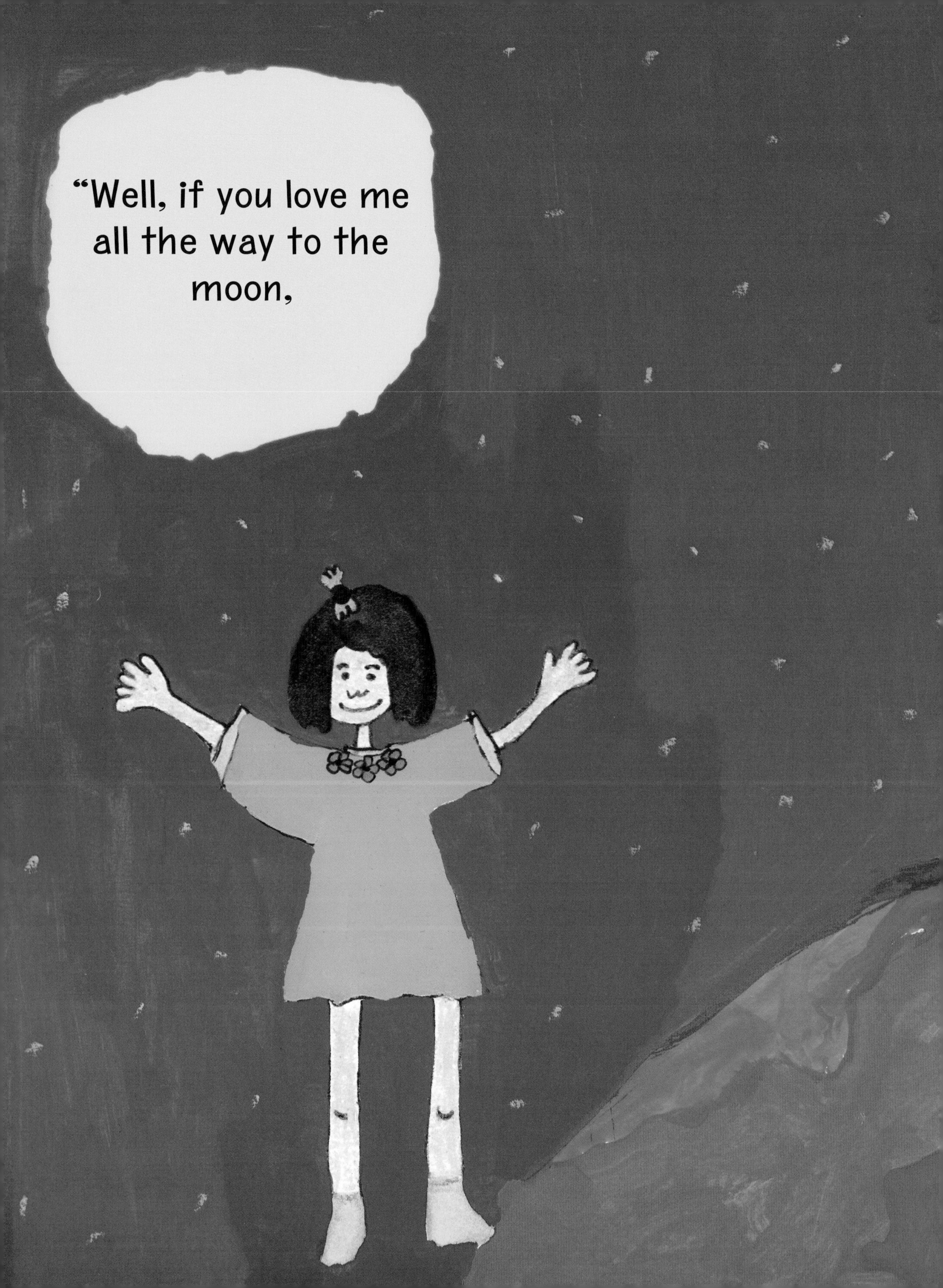

"Well, if you love me all the way to the moon,

then I love you
all the way to Pluto!"
Daddy knows all about space.
It was getting harder to beat him.

"Daddy, if you love me
all the way to Pluto,
then I love you
all the way to the stars."
For the first time
Daddy didn't answer right
away, but then he smiled
that smile that says
he knows he's going
to win.

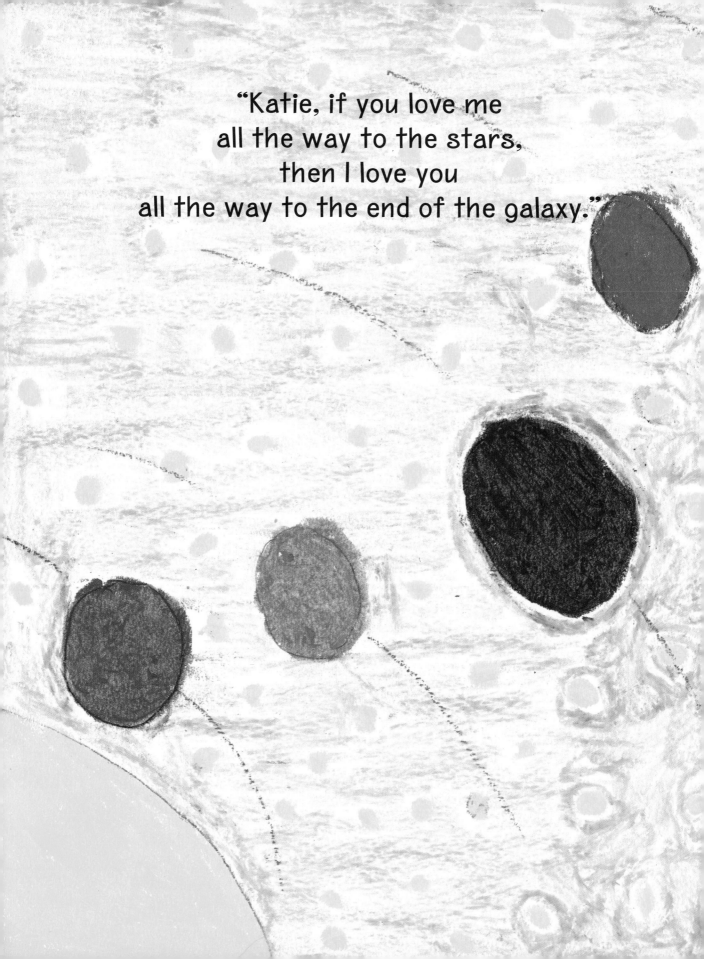

"Katie, if you love me
all the way to the stars,
then I love you
all the way to the end of the galaxy."

Oh, boy!
I didn't know what a galaxy was,
but it sure sounded big and far.
I knew I still loved
my daddy even more.

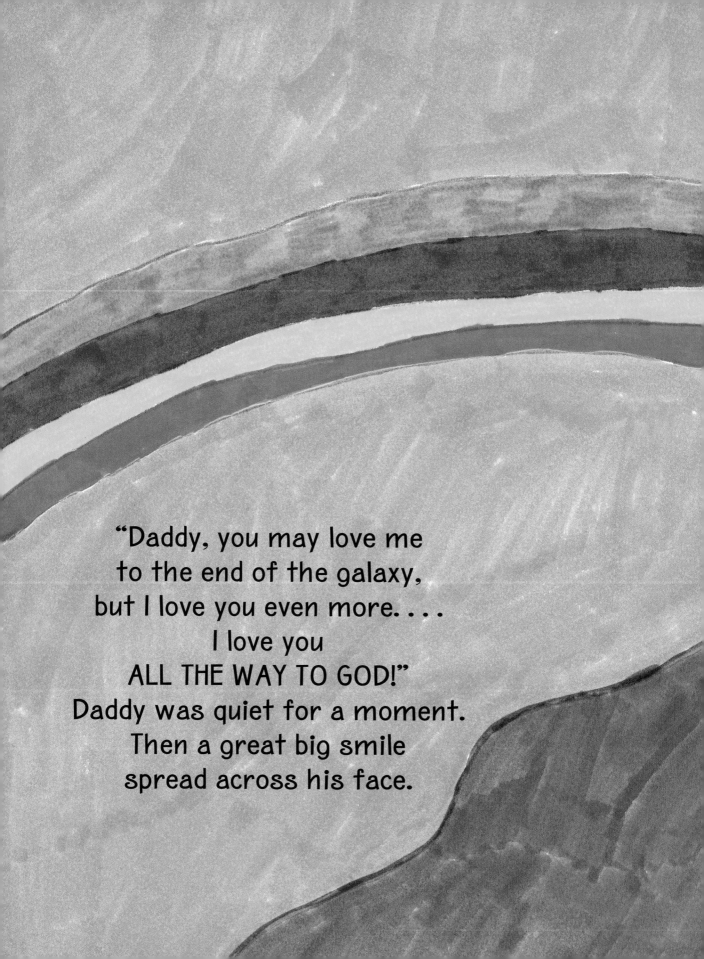

"Daddy, you may love me
to the end of the galaxy,
but I love you even more. . . .
I love you
ALL THE WAY TO GOD!"
Daddy was quiet for a moment.
Then a great big smile
spread across his face.

"Katie, that is the most beautiful thing
I've ever heard!
That's as far as love can go!
I love you too, Katie.
And I love you all the way to God!"

Now each night,
when our family goes to bed,
Daddy asks us all his loving question,
"How much does Daddy love you?"
and we all know the answer....

ALL THE WAY TO GOD!

All The Way To God is a true story.

When Katie Giuliano was four years old, she and her father started a bedtime word game. Each night, they went back and forth, trying to top each other in expressions of love. One night Katie captured the essence of love when she told her dad she loved him all the way to God. For the Giuliano Family, where God plays a central role, loving all the way to God became a favorite line for family and friends alike.

The story evolved into a book when "Dad" Giuliano was asked to create a special project for a graduate course on children's reading at St. Peter's College in New Jersey. Using Katie's words, he encouraged his five children to participate. The Giuliano children all worked on the illustrations, with the guidance of their creative mom, and helped their father write and edit the text. It was truly a family project, and it was a joy for Golden Books to publish the story.